# Guitar Pedal Mastery
## *Tone Secrets and Effect Chain Techniques Revealed*

# Table of Contents

# Chapter 1. Introduction

Unlock the door to a whole new realm of sonic opportunities with our Special Report on "Guitar Pedal Mastery: Tone Secrets and Effect Chain Techniques Revealed". This comprehensive guide is your passport to a world where you become the master conductor of your own musical symphony, wielding the power of tone and effect to craft a sound that is uniquely yours. Whether a novice just discovering the allure of guitar pedals or a seasoned musician seeking to expand their tonal palette, this report reveals secrets that transform the mystery of guitar pedals into your own tool for musical innovation. Don't miss the chance to elevate your music to dizzying new heights, fueling your creative expression with expert insights and practical tips—a compelling chorus of knowledge that is as enjoyable to read as it is invaluable to implement. Let your sound journey unfold; our Special Report is here to take you to the next level.

# Chapter 2. Understanding Pedals: An Introduction to Their Significance

In the thrilling world of live and recorded music, guitar pedals play a vital role, bridging the space between the musician and the audience. At first glance, these devices may seem daunting with their assortment of knobs, switches, and multicolored cables. Yet, once you gain a deeper understanding of their functionality, they become essential tools in shaping your sound.

## 2.1. The Essence of Guitar Pedals

Guitar pedals, also termed as stompboxes, are electronic units that alter and enhance the tonal output of an electric guitar in countless ways. They operate by conditioning the signal from a guitar before it reaches the amplifier, allowing musicians to adjust, modulate and distort their sound in a variety of creative ways. Guitar pedalboards, composed of multiple pedals, let the musician stack effects. This essentially allows a single instrumental voice to diversify into a whole orchestra of tones.

The usage of guitar pedals extends beyond mere tonal alteration, as these tools also have a transformative impact on the artistic approach and development of a musician. They enable the guitarist to experiment with nuanced aspects of their music and provide a platform to develop their own signature sound. By understanding and mastering pedal usage, guitarists can instinctively express their emotions through the music, creating more profound connections with the audience.

## 2.2. Pedal Categories

To help understand the vast universe of guitar pedals, we can categorize them into the following broad groups:

1. Distortion Pedals: These include overdrive, distortion, and fuzz pedals. They are essential for blues, rock, and metal genres, manipulating the sound to provide anything from a light crunch to a high gain roar.

2. Modulation Pedals: Incorporating chorus, flanger, and phaser effects, these pedals add depth and movement, creating a sense of space and dimension in the sound.

3. Time-Based Pedals: Including delay and reverb effects, these pedals give the illusion of playing in different environments such as a concert hall or a massive stadium, adding mood and character to the sound.

4. Filters and Equalization Pedals: These provide precise control over the frequency spectrum of the guitar signal, allowing the guitarist to boost or cut specific frequency ranges delivering a highly customized tone.

5. Miscellaneous Pedals: Other diverse effects like loopers, pitch shifters, octave pedals, and more fall under this category, offering endless opportunities for sonic exploration.

Each of these categories encompasses a myriad of everyday sounds we hear on our favorite tracks, lending them life and texture.

## 2.3. Anatomy of a Pedal

To understand how guitar pedals function, it's helpful to become familiar with their general structure. Though the specifics may vary from pedal to pedal, the following are common features you might find:

1. Footswitch: This is the key control mechanism, used to activate or deactivate the effect.

2. Input Jack: This is where the guitar signal enters the pedal.

3. Output Jack: The signal, with the effect applied, is directed to the amplifier from this point.

4. Knobs: These control the various parameters of the given effect, allowing you to tweak your sound.

5. Indicator Light: This LED light signals when the effect is active.

Through the deft maneuvering of these components, the guitarist can create a wide range of tones, from subtle colorations to drastic transformations.

# 2.4. Crafting Your Sound

Crafting a unique sound is a journey of personal exploration. By leveraging the potential of guitar effects, musicians can create their unique sonic identity. Many legendary guitarists have understood this, pioneering iconic sounds by creative usage and sometimes even misuse of guitar pedals.

Recognizing the type and order of effects can significantly impact the outcome. For instance, placing a delay pedal before a distortion pedal will yield a very different sound than placing the distortion before the delay. This ordering of pedals, often referred as pedal chain or signal chain, is an important variable to consider in your tonal expedition.

The process of understanding and mastering guitar pedals necessitates patience, experimentation, and an open mind. It's a dynamic dance between the logical and the creative, the technical and the emotive. As you experiment, bear in mind that there are no hard and fast rules. The pursuit is not for the perfect sound. It is for YOUR sound.

This brief overview serves as your springboard into a comprehensive and rewarding process of exploration in the world of guitar pedals. As you dive deeper, be prepared to discover the extraordinary capabilities of these small, boxy contraptions, shaping them into your personal set of symphonic tools. Remember, at the very heart of it, the pedal is simply an extension of your artistic voice. Harness its power wisely, and let it amplify not only your sound but also your musical soul.

# Chapter 3. The Art of Tone: Core Elements and Sound Sculpting

To truly understand and master the art of using guitar pedals, one must first comprehend the fundamental elements of tone and sound sculpting. Pulling together the strands of waveforms, frequencies, harmonics, and human hearing, we create aural landscapes that can evoke a spectrum of responses from ecstasy to contemplation. When aiming for perfection, subtle tweaks to your knobs and finely tuned adjustments can lead to vast transformations in your output.

## 3.1. Mapping Out the Sound Spectrum

Every guitarist should understand the sound spectrum—fundamental to all aspects of sound and music. View it as a spectrum of frequencies that comprise the entirety of human hearing, ranging from 20 Hz to 20 kHz. On the spectrum, your highs (treble), mids, and lows (bass) sit. Sculpting sound involves manipulating this spectrum to place your desired tones where you want and need them to be.

### 3.1.1. Lofty Highs, Sturdy Mids, and Heavy Lows

Bass frequencies serve as the foundation of your tone. They provide depth and warmth, occupying the range from approximately 20 to 250 Hz. Mid frequencies (250 Hz to 4 kHz) carry the meat of the sound, the core. They characterize a vast array of emotions and provide the bulk of tonal distinction. Treble frequencies (4 kHz to 20 kHz) offer crispness and clarity—responsible for the 'biting' tones and 'airy' sparkle.

When dialing in your tone, remember to visualize the sound spectrum and consider how your bass, mid, and treble frequencies will occupy this space.

# 3.2. The Role of Your Guitar and Amp

Before wedging any pedals in your chain, remember that the guitar and amp are major components of your tone. The pickups on your guitar (whether they be single-coil or humbuckers) have a significant bearing on your sound, producing different EQs and output levels. The amplifier, on the other hand, conditions and amplifies the signal, often adding its distinct character to the overall tone.

An understanding of your guitar's capabilities and your amplifier's characteristics ensures you start with a strong base tone—aesthetic and complementary to the sound you intend to create using pedals.

# 3.3. An Overview of Guitar Effect Types

Guitar effects usually fall under several categories—dynamics, filters, gain, modulation, time, and pitch. Each category offers unique ways to manipulate your original signal, providing unique tonal colors and textures.

### 3.3.1. Dynamics Effects

Dynamics effects manage the volume levels of your guitar signal. They include compressors, limiters, noise gates, and expanders. Compression, for instance, can be an invaluable tool, keeping your levels consistent and adding sustain to your notes.

### 3.3.2. Filter Effects

Filters modify your frequency response, allowing certain frequencies to pass while suppressing others. They include equalizers (EQs), wah-wah pedals, and phasers.

### 3.3.3. Gain-Based Effects

Gain effects such as boosters, overdrives, distortions, and fuzz pedals manipulate the amplitude of your signal, selectively clipping your signal to create everything from a gentle warmth to an aggressive roar.

### 3.3.4. Modulation Effects

Modulation effects add movement and depth to your tone. Examples include chorus, flanger, and tremolo pedals. They create their distinctive 'wavering' soundscapes by duplicating your signal and changing properties like speed, pitch, or time.

### 3.3.5. Time-Based Effects

These include delay and reverb effects, creating echoes and spaces, respectively. They replicate the experiences of playing in different environments—from tight rooms to large halls.

### 3.3.6. Pitch Effects

Octavers, Whammy, Harmonizer—these change the pitch of your signal, creating interesting layers and harmonic content.

# 3.4. Sculpting Your Sound with Pedals

The combination and arrangement of pedals play crucial roles in sculpting your tone. Placement can drastically affect your resulting sound.

A classic arrangement may follow this pattern: Dynamics (Compression) → Gain → Modulation → Time-based. However, rules are made to be broken. Once you're comfortable, experiment with the arrangement. Remember that art isn't about doing things by the book. The pedalboard setup that works for you is the one that achieves the sound you're after.

# 3.5. Practical Tips for Tone Exploration

Embrace the journey of tone discovery. Perfecting your tone isn't a linear process. It involves considerable experimentation—the route is seldom direct.

Remember this bit of advice: Slower is faster. Take your time to understand how individual pedals alter your tone. Controlled, deliberate changes encourage nuanced comprehension over wide-swinging adjustments.

Furthermore, learn to trust your ears. Lists of frequency ranges and pedal descriptions are useful guides, but your sound aligns with your personal taste. A pedal's value does not lie in its specs but in the services it renders to your music.

And finally, don't be afraid of the volume knob on your guitar. Manipulating it plays a huge role in your tone. Roll the knob back to clean your signal, and up to introduce gain and saturation. Introduce your pedals to different degrees of input gain by varying your guitar's volume.

In conclusion, sound sculpting and tone crafting is an infinite field of possibilities bounded only by imagination. Understanding these basic essentials lays the groundwork for your journey. Enjoy the ride!

# Chapter 4. Unlocking Pedal Functions: A Comprehensive Walkthrough

Before we turn our focus towards the seemingly infinite combinations and arrangements possible with guitar pedals, it's crucial to comprehend the individual components at play. Each effect pedal plays a distinct role in crafting your sound, and understanding their nuances is a significant stride toward mastering your sonic ensemble.

## 4.1. Understanding Your Pedal Types

Distortion, Overdrive, and Fuzz Pedals: The sonic trinity of hard rock and metal genres, these types of pedals alter the signal from your guitar to produce a distorted effect.

- Distortion pedals boost your signal's gain to make it louder and distorted. They give your sound a heavy, saturated crunch.

- Overdrive pedals also add gain, but less saturated than distortion. They emulate the naturally distorted sound of a tube amp pushed to its limits.

- Fuzz pedals drastically alter your sound to create a highly distorted, fuzzy, and sustain-rich effect. They're less concerned with emulating a natural amplifier sound and more with crafting an aggressive, unique tone.

Modulation Pedals: Here come the chorus, flanger and phaser effects you often hear in psychedelic and rock music.

- Chorus pedals make your signal sound fuller and richer. They achieve this by creating copies of your signal and slightly delaying and altering their pitch.

- Flanger pedals work similarly but with a shorter delay. Some describe the effect as a "jet plane" sound.

- Phaser pedals split your signal into two and change one part's phase. The result is a sweeping, otherworldly sound.

Time and Ambient Effect Pedals: Delay and Reverb pedals fall into this category. They add space and dimension to your music.

- Delay pedals repeat your signal like an echo, creating an illusion of your sound playing in a large space.

- Reverb pedals replicate different room sounds and ambient spaces. They can be used subtly for a touch of liveliness or drastically for an atmospheric sound.

# 4.2. Dialing In Your Settings

One of the first things you will notice on your pedals are various knobs or dials controlling different aspects of the effect. While the specific settings can vary from pedal to pedal, most fall into three general categories:

- Level or Volume: This determines how loudly the effect is being heard in your signal.

- Tone or EQ: These knobs allow you to shape the color of your tone, making it brighter or darker.

- Gain or Drive: These controls determine how intense the effect will be. For distortion or overdrive, it will control how "dirty" your signal gets.

Playing around with these knobs will give you a great feel for interacting with your pedals. Try extreme settings to dramatically hear the differences, then slowly dial back to find the sweet spot.

# 4.3. Experimenting With Pedal Order

The order of your pedals in the effect chain can significantly impact your sound. A commonly recommended order is: Filters (wah, auto-wah), Compressors, Pitch Shifters, Boost effects (overdrive, distortion, fuzz), Modulation effects (chorus, flanger, phaser, tremolo), Time-based effects (delay, reverb).

However, rules are meant to be broken. Don't hesitate to experiment with different combinations and orders. Your unique order could become "your sound".

Conclusion: Arriving here, you have now unlocked the first door to your pedal mastery. Now that you understand the world of pedals and their characteristics, you're ready to experiment and discover your unique guitar sound. In the next section, we'll further explore pairing different pedals and crafting even more unique soundscapes. Remember, as with any art form, the rules are merely guidelines. The most important thing is to explore, have fun, and create a sound that speaks to you.

# Chapter 5. Effect Chain Secrets: The Order that Makes a Difference

To experiment with and ultimately master the art of pedal effects, it's crucial to gain a deep understanding of the effect chain. This pivotal component determines how different effects interact with each other, shaping the combined output of your effects pedals and profoundly influencing your individual sonic signature.

## 5.1. The Basics of Pedal Order

The order in which you place your pedals plays a fundamental role in determining the end sound you achieve. Most guitarists adhere to a recommended order, which serves as a reliable starting point. However, remember that rules are meant to be broken - creativity and personal preferences often lead to unique and groundbreaking innovations.

The traditional, most commonly used order for guitar pedals is as follows:

1. Tuner
2. Compressor
3. Distortion / Overdrive
4. Modulation (Chorus, Flanger, Phaser)
5. Delay
6. Reverb

This sequence isn't random but is instead based on logical principles regarding how different effects interact with and influence each other. For example, you'll usually want your tuner at the beginning to receive an unaltered signal from your guitar, making tuning easier and more accurate.

## 5.2. Exploring Effect Interactions

Understanding how different effects interact can give you creative new ideas for pedal order. For instance, placing a reverb pedal before a distortion pedal will result in a severely distorted reverb sound, which may or may not be what you're aiming for.

Consider the interaction between a distortion and a delay pedal: If the distortion comes before the delay, each echoed note will be distorted. Conversely, if the delay comes before the distortion, the entire signal, including all echoes, will be distorted together. Both options can be valuable, depending on the desired sound.

## 5.3. Going Beyond the Standard: Workflow-Based Arrangement

While the standard pedal order we previously mentioned works great for most, there are valid reasons to diverge from this approach. A 'workflow-based arrangement' is an alternative setup based on your live playing needs and preferences.

For example, suppose you regularly engage and disengage your compressor and overdrive at the same time during performances. In such a case, placing these two pedals next to each other, regardless of 'standard order,' might make more ergonomic sense for you.

## 5.4. Buffering and True Bypass

Buffering and true bypass are critical considerations for effect chain setup. Buffering can help maintain signal strength through long cable runs, while true bypass keeps your unaffected signal 'pure.'

If all your pedals are true bypass, you may want to place a buffered pedal first in your chain to strengthen the signal that the rest of your pedals receive. Meanwhile, having a few buffered pedals scattered throughout your chain can prevent any potential tone loss from long cable runs, especially on stage.

# 5.5. The Power of Experimentation

Lastly, it becomes essential to highlight the power of experimentation. By trying out different pedal orders, you may stumble upon unique soundscapes that resonate with your musical style.

This wraps up our deep exploration of pedal chains and their sheer importance in shaping your tone and sound. As you can see, much of this involves not just an understanding of the principles at play, but a willingness to experiment beyond the 'rules.' So plug in, tune up, and let your creativity guide your tone journey.

# Chapter 6. Dialing the Perfect Tone: Fine-tuning Your Pedals

Tone—such an elusive yet integral concept in the realm of music. The instrument we use to produce sound plays a vital role, and in the land of guitar tones, effects pedals ascend that tone to entirely new dimensions. Fine-tuning these devices is essential to truly express your musical soul, and here's exactly how.

## 6.1. Understanding Your Pedals

To navigate the world of guitar effects pedals, it's essential to know what you're working with. The two most common pedal types are analog and digital. Analog pedals comprise of physical circuitry and electronic components which sculpt your raw guitar signal. Digital ones use programmed algorithms, which afford a wide range of effects, from the replication of analog pedal sounds to complex modulation effects.

Analog pedals possess a more natural and authentic feel, while digital pedals offer versatility. Understanding the nature of your pedals is the starting point of this tuning journey.

## 6.2. Acquainting With The Tone Parameters

Every guitar pedal has an array of knobs or sliders that can be adjusted. Here are some common oncs:

- Gain or Drive: Determines the intensity of the effect. Applies to distortion, overdrive, fuzz pedals, and certain modulation effects.

- Level or Volume: Controls the output level of the effect signal.

- Tone, EQ, or Filter: Modifies tone color or sound quality.

- Mix or Blend: Dictates the amount of dry (unaffected) vs wet (affected) signal.

- Speed or Rate: Sets the pace of time-based effects such as tremolo or chorus.

- Depth: Governs the intensity of time-based or modulation effects.

## 6.2.1. Fine-Tuning Distortion, Overdrive, and Fuzz Pedals

More distortion doesn't per se result in a better or louder sound. Begin with the lowest setting. Gradually increase Gain for a richer overdrive or distortion, and stop when it begins to overpower your tone.

Tone or EQ let you shape your tone's character. For example, boosting low frequencies gives a fuller tone, emphasizing highs provides a sharper, edgier feel.

The Level or Volume should ideally match the volume of your unaltered signal. To prevent sudden volume drops or surges when the pedal is switched on, test the setting with other pedals in the chain.

## 6.2.2. Working with Modulation Pedals

Modulation effects usually have Rate and Depth knobs. They affect the character and strength of your sound but can easily make it unlistenable when abused.

Maintain a subtle approach. Set Depth and Rate to the minimum, then tweak gently until the modulation enriches the tone without masking it. This will ensure your core tone remains recognizable.

Combine effects carefully. Stacking numerous modulation pedals can lead to a very complex and possibly unpleasant sound. Make changes sparingly, always remembering each pedal adds its own color.

### 6.2.3. Using Delay and Reverb Pedals

Delay and reverb pedals create repeats or reflections of your sound, adding depth and dimension.

Start with Mix or Level adjustments. At the lowest, the effect will not be heard. As you increase the setting, the effect becomes more apparent. As with other pedals, ensure the effect level matches your guitar's dry level.

Time or Delay sets the delay timing or reverb size. For delay pedals, this controls the distance between each echo. For reverbs, it imparts scope to your reverb—smaller values equating to smaller rooms, larger ones to concert halls.

# 6.3. Order of Pedals in the Chain

The order in which you place your pedals significantly influences the final tone. Although it's often a matter of personal preference and experimentation, here's a standard order to guide you:

1. Tuner: Allows precise tuning unaffected by other pedals.

2. Wah or EQ: Wah modifies specific frequencies, while EQ helps to tailor your tone.

3. Compressor: Levels out your signal.

4. Distortion, Overdrive, or Fuzz: Adds gain before modulation.

5. Modulation Effects (Flanger, Phaser, Chorus): Modulates the distorted signal.

6. Delay or Reverb: Applies delay/reverb to the modulated signal.

7. Volume Pedal: Controls the overall volume of your effect-laden signal.

# 6.4. Experiment and Document

Tone-hunting is as much about experimentation as knowing your gear. Take note of the settings that work for you. Recording your sessions can help you identify the desirable and tweak the less than perfect.

Resources like online communities, fellow musicians, and dedicated gear magazines offer invaluable insights into their setup secrets.

Your journey in crafting the perfect tone is bound to be a mesmerizing one, backed by knowledge and fuelled by creativity. Filter through the noise, seek your unique voice, and embrace the pleasure of fine-tuning your pedals. The subtlest knob twist could unveil an entirely new musical landscape. So, dare to explore, for music is your universe—unfurl it one pedal setting at a time!

# Chapter 7. Advanced Techniques: Stacking and Combining Effects

In the field of sonic exploration, one advanced method to create a truly unique tonal expression is through the skillful stacking and combining of effects. This concept, while not new to seasoned pedal enthusiasts, provides a universe of sound-scapes often unexplored by newcomers. Stacking involves running one pedal into another, while combining refers to the affair of blending or balancing multiple effects simultaneously to create entirely distinct tones.

## 7.1. Understanding Signal Flow

Before we delve into the subtler aspects of effect integration, it's crucial to understand signal flow. Essentially, signal flow is the path the guitar's sound takes from the moment it's played until it reaches the listener's ear. In simple terms, your guitar signal starts at the guitar strings, passes through your cables, pedals, amplifier, the air, and finally, concludes at the eardrum. However, the order in which your signal passes through various pedals (your signal chain) significantly impacts the final output.

Commonly, the pedal order follows this scheme: tuner, filter (including wah), compression, pitch shift, drive (overdrive, distortion, fuzz), modulation (chorus, flanger, phaser), time-based effects (delay, reverb), and volume/panning/ambience. This is, however, by no means an immutable rule. Exploring unconventional signal routes can yield unexpected and exciting results.

## 7.2. Experimenting with Stacking Order

Stacking refers to running one pedal into another, and the order in which the pedals are stacked is critical. Because each pedal interacts with the sound coming into it, the order in which they line up significantly shapes the outcome of your tone.

For instance, if you use a reverb pedal followed by a distortion pedal, the distortion will amplify the reverberated signal, resulting in potentially chaotic and uncontrollable fuzz. Conversely, placing the distortion before the reverb allows the reverb to act on the distorted signal instead, creating a more controlled, room-filling sound.

Always remember that there is no definitive right or wrong when experimenting, the best sound is ultimately the one that matches your desired tonal identity. Explore different stacking sequences such as Distortion > Overdrive, Overdrive > Distortion, Modulation > Fuzz, Fuzz > Modulation, and others for fascinating combinations.

## 7.3. The Power of Gain-Staging

Gain staging refers to controlling the volume level at each stage of the signal path. It's an integral part of creating a balanced tone and avoiding noise like unwanted distortion or hiss. While stacking pedals, gain staging becomes even more vital.

For example, when stacking drive pedals, it's common practice to set the first pedal to boost the volume minimally or leave it unchanged and use the second pedal for most of the volume boost. This order prevents the first pedal from overpowering the second pedal, leading to an overstuffed tone or excessive noise.

Clarity often comes from constraining your gain stages. So, the general rule is to keep everything as clean as you can, until you get to the stage where you want to introduce deliberate distortion.

# 7.4. Combining Effects - Synergy and Contrast

While stacking refers to running one pedal into another, combining effects is more about achieving balance and harmony between different effects. Here, the emphasis lies not on the order, but how different pedals act together to refine your tone.

There are two main paths to tread here: synergy and contrast. Synergy implies using effects that complement each other, like combining a delay pedal and a reverb pedal to create an echoey, ambient soundscape or pairing a tremolo pedal with a phaser to create a swirling, pulsating effect.

On the other hand, contrast involves using effects that oppose each other — for instance, using a fuzz pedal for harmonic richness paired with a gated pedal to cut the decay short. The contrast can lead to unique and attention-grabbing tones.

# 7.5. Using Effect Loops and Multi-fx Pedals

Effect loops, typical in most amplifiers, allow you to decide whether your amp's preamp section is located before or after certain effects in the signal chain. For instance, modulation and time-based effects usually sound more organic when placed after the preamp. Experiment with the effects loop, as it can enhance your tone significantly.

If you're using a multi-effects pedal, you can save various effect combinations as presets. This component opens a whole new echelon of stacking and combining possibilities. For example, you can preset a combination of fuzz, delay, and wah for Solos, while another preset may combine chorus and overdrive for rhythm sections.

## 7.6. Subtle Settings for Dramatic Discoveries

Lastly, remember not to overlook the power of subtle adjustments. Even minor changes in pedal settings can lead to considerable tonal shifts. For example, subtly adjusting the feedback settings on a delay pedal or the dwell settings on a reverb pedal can result in profound sonic differences. Be patient and open-minded, and you'll unearth new sonic treasures in your journey.

In conclusion, stacking and combining effects is an advanced technique, and like all such techniques, mastery requires exploring, listening, and refining. With patience, practice, and an open ear, you will be well on your way to carving out a unique and compelling sonic identity that amplifies your creative expression.

# Chapter 8. Blend Magic: Creating Unique Sounds with Pedals

Often, the allure of music does not reside in the individual elements but in the blend—a unique commixture of sounds that creates an unmistakable, captivating sonic signature. This section is dedicated to demonstrating how you can combine different guitar pedals to create such an alluring soundscape. This is a journey of discovery, where no path is wrong, and the sonic destination is entirely at your discretion.

## 8.1. Demystifying Pedal Types

Before you can paint a sonic masterpiece, you need to understand your colors. In the world of guitar pedals, each pedal type is a different color—each adding its own charm and characteristic to your tone. There are various kinds of pedals, each lending its unique flavor.

Distortion, Overdrive, and Fuzz: These pedals add harmonic content to your signal, lending aggression, sustain, and grit. They are fantastic for creating a plug-and-play lead tone and for energizing your chords with extra bite.

Modulation: These pedals (chorus, flanger, phaser) add undulating, swirling richness to your tone, creating an impression of space and movement. They are excellent for textural rhythm parts and lush, expansive guitar solos.

Delay and Reverb: These echo-based pedals add a sense of depth, making your guitar sound as if it's in a vast room or space. They are the secret sauce for producing a full, "epic" guitar sound.

Filtering and EQ: These pedals alter the frequency response of your guitar, carving out or boosting specific frequency ranges. Use them to control how your guitar nestles into a mix or to achieve certain tonal characteristics.

## 8.2. Pedal Order Matters

The sequence in which your guitar pedals are ordered, known as the signal chain, can profoundly impact your tone. Although there are no absolute rules, the conventional wisdom suggests the following order: Dynamics > Pitch > Boost > Modulation > Time.

The idea is simple: start with the pedals that affect the signal at the source (compressors, pitch shifters), go through the pedals that shape the tone (overdrive, EQ), add color with modulation pedals, and lastly, apply time-related effects (delay, reverb). This sequence usually preserves the integrity of the original signal.

## 8.3. Matrimony of Tonality: Pedal Pairings

There are certain pedal pairings that have withstood the test of time, and these renowned combinations can serve as your initial sonic experiments. Here are a few:

Overdrive and Delay: Think of iconic lead tones that soar and sustain. An overdrive pedal ensures your solos can cut through the mix, while delay adds spaciousness and complexity.

Chorus and Reverb: A textbook recipe for crafting an ethereal, crystal-clean soundscape. This combination conjures an expansive, shimmering wall of sound, ideal for intros, outros, or ambient parts.

Fuzz and Wah: This pairing has been gracing gnarly rock riffs for decades. Fuzz adds monstrous, flabby textures, while the wah pedal helps highlight specific frequencies and gives your tone a vocal-like quality.

# 8.4. Creating Your Unique Blend

It's essential to grasp that the real tone magic happens when you go beyond established norms and venture into uncharted territories. Bring out your inner sonic alchemist by experimenting with the order and settings of your pedals. Use EQ to shape your fuzz tone, add a dash of chorus to your overdriven signal, feed your modulated sound into a tight, slapback delay.

Nothing should prevent you from disobeying conventional pedal sequences. It is only by veering off the beaten track that you might stumble upon an elusive, enchanting tone—your own unique sonic fingerprint.

These are merely some tips and guidelines to get you started on your path to becoming a conductor of your own symphonic masterpiece. The most liberating aspect of working with guitar pedals is that there is no right or wrong way to do it. It's all about personal expression; your guitar, your pedals, your sound. This journey is yours and yours alone—embrace it and enjoy the ride.

# 8.5. Conclusion

Mastering guitar pedals and creating unique sounds could be considered an art on its own. Each pedal adds a brushstroke to the canvas of your tone, each adjustment imbues your sound with audacious colors or intimate shades. By understanding the mechanics of each pedal and experimenting with pedal chains, you give yourself the freedom to paint original sonic landscapes that express your unique musical vision. And therein lies the magic: When it all comes together, it's not just about the technicalities but how those all-encompassing elements, when combined, tell your story, in your voice.

# Chapter 9. Insider's Guide: Mastering Delay and Reverb

Delay and reverb effects play a huge role in shaping the tone and character of a guitar's output. When used skillfully, they can add depth and spaciousness to your music, emulate different acoustic environments, and create mesmerizing soundscapes. Let's delve into the details, equipping you with the understanding and techniques to harness the full potential of these effects.

## 9.1. Understanding Delay

One of the mainstays of a guitarist's pedalboard, delay is a time-based effect that replicates your guitar's input and plays it back after a set period of time, creating an "echo" effect. The parameters of a delay pedal afford you a variety of controls, each altering the character of the echo in its own unique way.

- *Delay Time:* Dictates the period between the original signal and the repeated signal.

- *Feedback:* Controls the number of repeats — a low feedback setting will produce fewer echoes, while a high setting could generate a virtually endless series of repeats.

- *Mix:* Balances the volume of the original signal (dry) and the delayed signal (wet).

Now, let's explore three prevalent types of delay:

1. Analog Delay: This uses an analog circuit to produce a warm, slightly deteriorated echo. They are loved for their characteristic tonal decay compared to digital delay pedals, which reproduce the input signal exactly.

2. Digital Delay: As touched on above, digital delay pedals produce a

pristine, exact copy of the input signal. These are equipped with longer delay times and often include tap tempo features and subdivision options.

3. Tape Echo: This delay type is an early form of analog delay which uses magnetic tape to record and playback the signal. Well known for its unique warm and organic tone.

# 9.2. Practical Delay Techniques and Applications

Delay can be used in some very creative ways to enhance your playing. Here are some tried and true techniques:

- *Slapback:* This is a type of very short delay often used in country and rockabilly genres. It's characterized by a single repeat with a fast delay time (around 100-200ms), and no or very short feedback.

- *Doubling:* Here, you use delay to create a fuller sound by making it seem like two guitars are playing at once. Keep the delay time short and the feedback at zero.

- *Ambient Swells:* Commonly used in ambient and worship genres, this involves swelling the guitar's volume after striking the note or chord with a longer delay time and higher feedback.

# 9.3. Understanding Reverb

Reverb emulates the natural echo that happens when sound waves bounce off walls, floor, and ceiling. It's an incredibly powerful tool for guitarists, as it provides a sense of space and ambience to your playing. The parameters on a reverb pedal are notably similar to those on delay pedals. However, the parameters are more about defining the size, decay, and tonal quality of the simulated space, rather than timing the repetition of the 'echo'.

# 9.4. Practical Reverb Techniques and Applications

Here are some essential techniques for using reverb effectively in your music:

- *Tight Room Ambience:* Setting a small room size with a short decay creates a sense of intimacy, great for solo fingerstyle work.

- *Large Hall Reverb:* This is great for slow, melodic lead lines. Crank up the room size and decay time to create a lush, ethereal timbre.

- *Gated Reverb:* Popular in the '80s, gated reverb is when the reverb effect abruptly cuts off after a certain threshold, giving a unique, synthetic quality to the sound.

Finally, keep in mind that while these effects can add a lot to your sound, they can also quickly make things messy when used excessively. As with most things in music - and life - balance is key.

By investing time in understanding these effects and experimenting with different settings and techniques, you will be able to explore new sonic territories, opening up a world of expressive possibilities that you may have not thought possible.

# Chapter 10. Sculpting Distortion: Mastery over the Beast

In the realm of guitar effects pedals, few concepts are as central and impactful as distortion. Distortion molds the guitar's primal sound, shaping it into a formidable beast or a gentle creature to enhance the emotional contour of your music. But how do we tame this beast? How do we transform it into a willing accomplice in our musical adventures? The answer lies not only in technical proficiency but also in a deep and intuitive understanding of the myriad possibilities that distortion offers.

## 10.1. Understanding Distortion

To control distortion, we must first understand it. At its most basic, distortion fundamentally alters the clean guitar signal by adding harmonic complexity and clipping the audio signal. This clipping effect leads to a distinctive 'crunch' or 'fuzzy' sound, a sonic component that has become an integral part of genres like rock, metal, punk, and blues.

There are three broad categories of distortion: overdrive, distortion, and fuzz. Overdrive produces a warm, natural, and slightly clipped tone. It emulates the sound of tube amplifiers pushed to their limit and is often used in blues and rock. The Distortion pedal produces a harder, more aggressive sound - a staple for heavy rock and metal. Fuzz is the most extreme form; it radically transforms the signal, giving a saturated, buzzy tone ideal for Stoner Rock and Psychadelic music.

# 10.2. Harnessing the Power of Distortion Pedals

Turning to pedals' practical application, here's a step-by-step guide on how to make the most of your distortion pedal:

1. Select the right distortion pedal: Each pedal has a unique character that conveys a different atmosphere. Try different overdrive, distortion, and fuzz pedals to discover one suitable for your musical style.

2. Fine-tune the Gain: Vary the distortion level using the Gain control. Lower settings create a mellow, bluesy tone, while higher settings give a more aggressive, harder rock sound.

3. Calibrate the Tone/EQ: Adjust the tone or EQ settings to shape the frequency response of your sound. Experiment with these controls to achieve the perfect balance.

4. Adjust the Volume/Level: Set the overall output with the Volume or Level control. A higher setting can push your amp harder, creating interesting interactions between pedal and amplifier distortion.

# 10.3. The Art of Stacking Distortion Pedals

Once you master single pedal use, it's time to explore the versatile world of distortion stacking. Here, you combine two or more pedals to create complex, layered sounds. Applying this technique enhances your sonic palette, allowing you to sculpt tones unattainable with a single pedal.

However, stacking pedals without understanding the underlying principles can lead to tonal chaos rather than refinement. Follow these key guidelines for effective stacking:

1. Pedal Order Matters: Generally, pedals should be placed in order of gain staging, with lower-gain pedals (such as overdrive) going first and higher-gain pedals (like distortion or fuzz) following. This arrangement often yields musically pleasing results.

2. Experiment with Different Combinations: Don't be afraid to try unconventional combinations. Sometimes, placing a fuzz before an overdrive or a distortion before a boost can yield unique, exciting sounds.

3. Control Levels: Be mindful of each pedal's output level. Gradually increasing the level through the chain often provides better control and results in a more musical sound.

# 10.4. Secrets to Improving Distortion Tone

Garnering a world-class distortion tone doesn't simply boil down to gaining mastery over pedals. Many factors contribute to this goal, including guitar settings, amplifier tweaking, and even your playing technique. Here are some pointers:

1. Guitar Tone Controls: Don't overlook the impact your guitar's volume and tone knobs have on distortion. Experiment with these controls; sometimes, dialing back the guitar's volume can clean up the distortion and provide a wide range of textures.

2. Amplifier Settings: The settings of your amplifier significantly affect the resulting distortion tone. Experiment with various settings, but remember that often a 'cleaner', slightly less distorted setting allows for better articulation and note clarity.

3. Technique: Your playing style significantly impacts your distortion tone. Harder pick attack will yield a more aggressive tone, while softer picking or fingerpicking will often create a smoother, creamier distortion.

A mastery of distortion is a lifelong journey. Understanding the basics, experimenting fearlessly, and being open to the unexpected are the main steps on the path to gaining control over this formidable beast and bending it to your will. And remember, in the pursuit of tone, there's no right or wrong—only what works for you and what moves you and your listeners. Happy tone sculpting!

# Chapter 11. Final Touches: Maintaining Your Pedals

Maintaining your pedals is as important as the initial process of selecting and assembling your pedalboard. After all, your pedals are instrumental within your sound architecture. They warrant a meticulous care routine to keep them in top shape, assuring they deliver exceptional performance. Regular maintenance, right from cleaning your effects board to checking your power supply, provides you with a broad sonic palette, and protects against unforeseen hiccups during performances.

## 11.1. Cleaning Your Pedals

Pedals accumulate dust and dirt over time, compromising not only their aesthetic appearance but also potentially impairing their performance capability. Cleaning your pedals regularly does not just keep them aesthetically pleasing, but it can also enhance their longevity. However, remember to steer clear from abrasive materials and harsh cleaning chemicals.

Start by wiping your pedals gently with a soft, dry cloth to dust off any surface dirt. If need be, use a humid cloth for stubborn spots. Avoid soaking the pedals, as excess moisture can be detrimental to your pedal's electronic circuitry, potentially leading to malfunctions and short-circuits. Dry thoroughly after each cleaning session to ensure no water residue is left to evaporate naturally.

Electric contact cleaner is recommended for cleaning potentiometers, jacks, and switches. These areas can gather grime, affecting signal flow. However, such cleaners should be used sparingly and only after reading and following the manufacturer's guidelines.

Before using cleaning agents on your pedals, ensure you are in a well-ventilated area and wearing appropriate protection, such as gloves and goggles. Always switch off and unplug your pedals before attempting any cleaning procedures.

## 11.2. Checking and Replacing The Batteries

Although some guitarists power their pedals exclusively with power packs, many others use batteries. If you fall into the latter category, ensure you always have sufficient spare batteries on hand, especially during gigs.

Frequent monitoring of the batteries is paramount to avoid running out of power during a performance. Make sure to replace them when their power levels start becoming inconsistent or diminishing. Keeping track of how often you change your batteries can help you anticipate future replacements.

Never leave dead batteries inside a pedal. Old batteries can leak, causing corrosive substances to ruin your pedal's inner circuitry. If a battery leaks, act quickly to remove and clean the area to prevent any corrosive damage.

## 11.3. Checking Cables and Connections

Regularly review your cables to ensure they are functioning correctly. Over time, cables may degrade, which can bring about signal loss, hums, and noise. Check the cables' ends to see if they are firm, as loose cables can cause undesired static and signal loss.

Consider occasionally unplugging and plugging your pedals. Doing so can help scrape off any oxidization that might have formed on your jacks, thereby improving contact and signal quality.

If you're encountering issues that aren't resolvable through regular cleaning, consider hiring a professional service or utilizing your warranty, if still valid. Remember, DIY solutions might not always be suitable or safe, especially when dealing with intricate electronics and circuitry.

## 11.4. Regular Power Supply Check

Power supplies play a crucial role in the optimal functioning of your pedals. Whether you're using a battery-powered or a mains supply, conduct regular checks to prevent disruptions. For mains supplies, one useful tip is ensuring your power strips and cables are in good condition, not worn or frayed.

For batteries, as earlier mentioned, ensure they are replaced timely. A decline in performance may indicate a low-power battery, which warrants replacement.

## 11.5. Firmware Updates and Digital Interface Checks

Modern-day pedals sometimes come with digital interfaces and may require periodic firmware updates. Be sure to register your pedal with the manufacturer to receive updates and notifications about potential firmware changes. Install these updates as soon as possible to avoid any technical issues or compatibility problems.

In conclusion, the key to keeping your pedals in top condition relies on regular maintenance and routine checks. Not only will your pedals sound better, but they'll also last longer. Ultimately, this ensures that your sonic symphony continues to ring true, resonating with every strum on your guitar.

www.ingramcontent.com/pod-product-compliance
Lightning Source LLC
LaVergne TN
LVHW051630050326
832903LV00033B/4710